CAPE COD
Invasion!

Mark Penta

Commonwealth Editions
Beverly, Massachusetts

First edition

Cover and interior design by John Barnett at 4 Eyes Design
Author photo by Ted Murphy
Printed in Korea

Published by Commonwealth Editions, an imprint of Memoirs Unlimited, Inc.
266 Cabot Street, Beverly, Massachusetts 01915
Visit us on the Web at www.commonwealtheditions.com.

To learn more about Mark Penta and his artwork, visit www.markpenta.com.

To my parents, Rosemarie and Marshall,
for your constant support and for giving me the Cape!

Thanks to Webster Bull for editing the captions.
Thanks also to Ted, J4, Spencer, Cliff, and the Red Olives.

BOURNE

They arrive every summer, passing over the bridges in droves.

SANDWICH

Coming from far away, they feel as though they've landed in a different world.

FALMOUTH

Some just pass through on their way to the islands.

HYANNIS

As the Fourth of July approaches, harbor traffic soars.

DENNIS

At the peak of summer, many crowd the beaches.

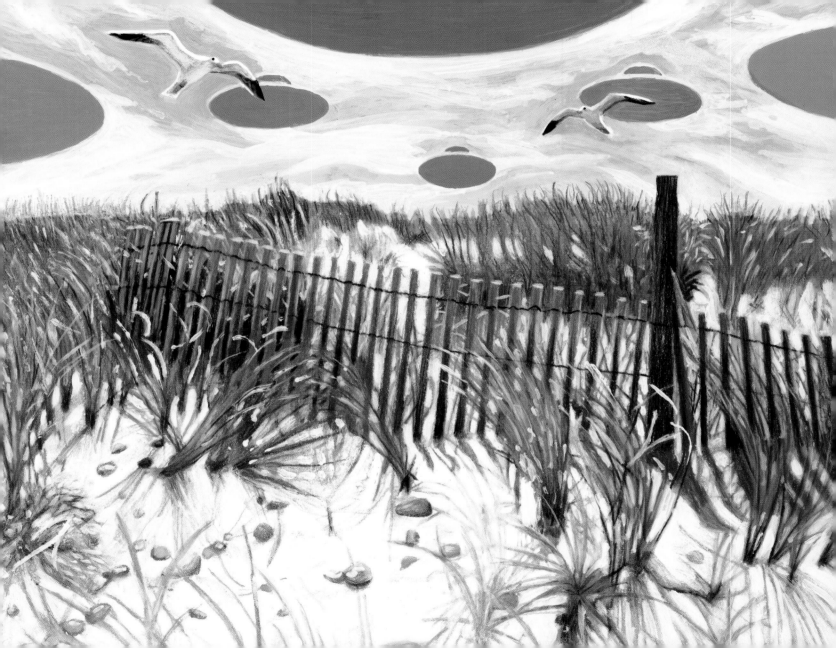

BREWSTER

Some will go any distance for ice cream.

HARWICH

There's something otherworldly about a moonlit night on the Cape.

CHATHAM

In broad daylight, few places on Earth look as charming.

ORLEANS

Seafood shacks and ocean breezes lure them toward the docks.

EASTHAM

Along the seashore, they squint in the heat and glare.

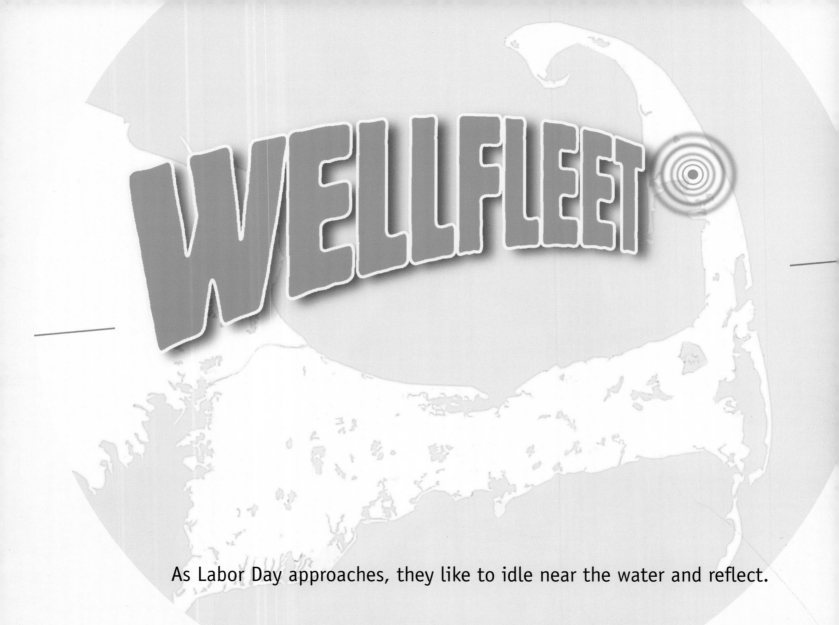

As Labor Day approaches, they like to idle near the water and reflect.

TRURO

Some prefer the solitude of the Outer Cape, where a couple can enjoy being alone.

PROVINCETOWN

What might seem alien elsewhere is accepted here.

After Labor Day they drift away, but like birds of passage they'll be back next year.

Mark Penta is a freelance illustrator and lifelong summer resident of Cape Cod. A University of Hartford Art School graduate, his work has appeared in *Alfred Hitchcock* and *Asimov* magazines. Young readers from New England might recognize his book cover art for T. M. Murphy's *Belltown Mystery Series*.

Mark teaches drawing and cartooning privately to kids and adults. He has also taught at Rhode Island School of Design, Dean College, Mass Bay College, and other schools. There's a good chance you've had your caricature drawn by Mark: he is one of Boston's premier caricaturists at private parties and corporate events. *Cape Cod Invasion!*, his first picture book, combines his passion for Cape Cod with his love of science fiction.